Nighttime Animals

FIRST EDITION
Series Editor Deborah Lock; **US Senior** Editor Shannon Beatty; **Art Director** Martin Wilson;
Designer Yamini Panwar; **Picture Researcher** Surya Sarangi;
Senior Producer, Pre-Production Ben Marcus; **Jacket Designer** Martin Wilson;
Reading Consultant Linda Gambrell, PhD

THIS EDITION
Editorial Management by Oriel Square
Produced for DK by WonderLab Group LLC
Jennifer Emmett, Erica Green, Kate Hale, *Founders*

Editors Grace Hill Smith, Libby Romero, Maya Myers, Michaela Weglinski;
Photography Editors Kelley Miller, Annette Kiesow, Nicole DiMella;
Managing Editor Rachel Houghton; **Designers** Project Design Company;
Researcher Michelle Harris; **Copy Editor** Lori Merritt; **Indexer** Connie Binder;
Proofreader Larry Shea; **Reading Specialist** Dr. Jennifer Albro; **Curriculum Specialist** Elaine Larson

Published in the United States by DK Publishing
1745 Broadway, 20th Floor, New York, NY 10019

Copyright © 2023 Dorling Kindersley Limited
DK, a Division of Penguin Random House LLC
23 24 25 26 10 9 8 7 6 5 4 3 2 1
001-334115-Sept/2023

A catalog record for this book
is available from the Library of Congress.
HC ISBN: 978-0-7440-7534-2
PB ISBN: 978-0-7440-7535-9

DK books are available at special discounts when purchased in bulk for sales promotions, premiums,
fundraising, or educational use. For details, contact: DK Publishing Special Markets,
1745 Broadway, 20th Floor, New York, NY 10019
SpecialSales@dk.com

Printed and bound in China

The publisher would like to thank the following for their kind permission to reproduce their images:
a=above; c=center; b=below; l=left; r=right; t=top; b/g=background

Dreamstime.com: Hotshotsworldwide 22c, Ondej Prosick 4-5, Tifonimages 28-29

Cover images: *Front:* **Dreamstime.com:** Krissikunterbunt b; **Shutterstock.com:** johnpluto tl, Propex;
Back: **Dreamstime.com:** Pavel Naumov cra

All other images © Dorling Kindersley
For more information see: www.dkimages.com

For the curious
www.dk.com

Nighttime Animals

Contents

6   Night Falls

8   Coyotes

10   Owls

12   Moths

14   Scorpions

16   Boa Constrictors

18   Lorises

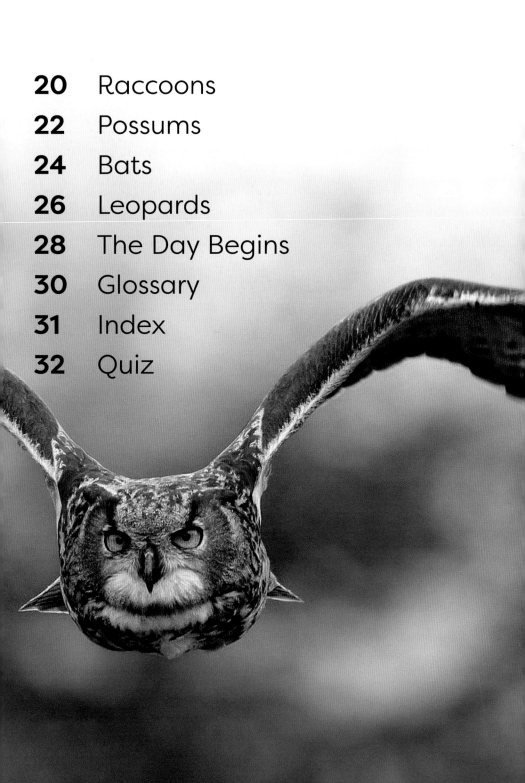

20 Raccoons

22 Possums

24 Bats

26 Leopards

28 The Day Begins

30 Glossary

31 Index

32 Quiz

Night Falls

The sun sets.
The nighttime animals
wake up.
It's time to eat.

Coyotes

Coyotes run and hunt.
They call to each other.

Owls

Owls look and listen.
Then they swoop in
to catch an animal.

wing

talon

Moths

Moths fly around
in the moonlight.

Scorpions

Scorpions lift
their stingers.
They are ready
to attack.

stinger

claw

Boa Constrictors

A boa constrictor slithers along a branch.

It searches
for food.

Lorises

Lorises see in the dark with wide-open eyes.

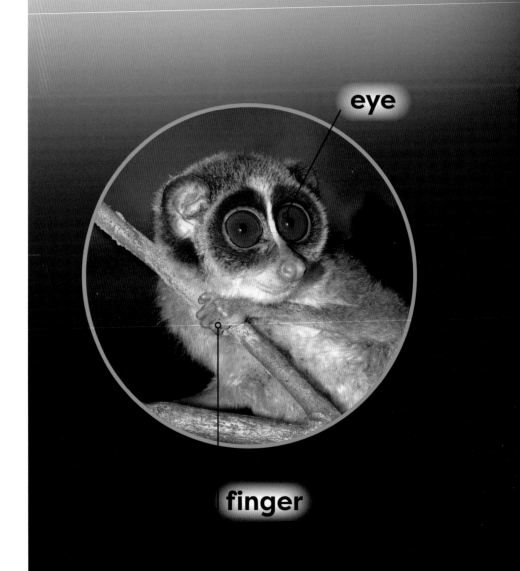

eye

finger

Raccoons

Raccoons scamper over logs.

They will eat any food they can find.

fur

Possums

Possums scurry around with their babies, called joeys.

joey

Bats

Bats fly around at night. They squeak through their noses.

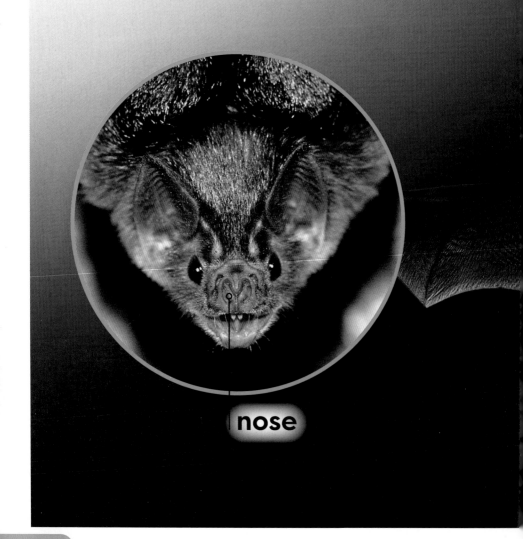

nose

Leopards

A leopard hunts alone. Its glowing eye scan see very well in the dark.

eye

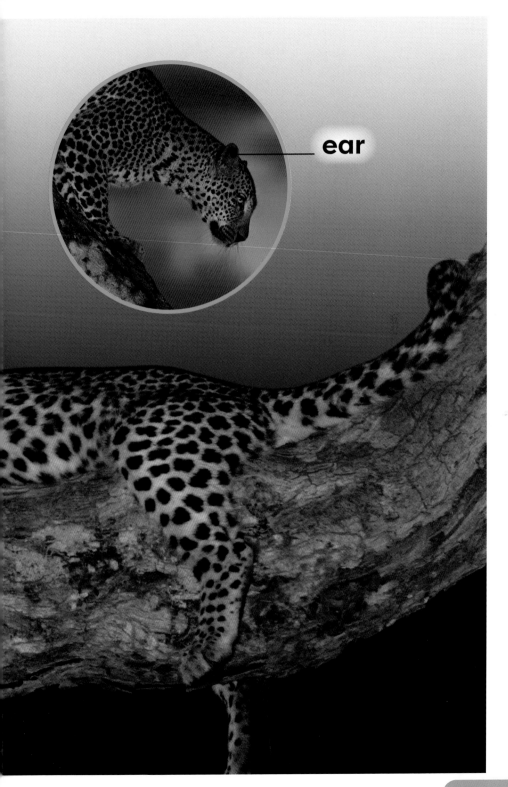

ear

The Day Begins

The sun rises.
The nighttime
animals sleep.
It's been a
busy night.

Glossary

fur
the hair that grows on the bodies of many mammals

joey
young possum

stinger
stinging part of an insect

talon
sharp claw of a bird

wing
arm of a bird covered with feathers

Index

bats   24

boa constrictors   16

claw   14

coyotes   8

ear   27

eyes   18, 26

finger   18

fur   21

joey   22

leopards   26

lorises   18

moths   12

nose   24

owls   10

possums   22

raccoons   20

scorpions   14

sleep   28

stinger   14

talon   11

wake up   6

wing   10

Quiz

Answer the questions to see what you have learned. Check your answers with an adult.

1. Which animal uses a stinger to attack?

2. Which animal has wide-open eyes to see in the dark?

3. Which animal eats any food it can find?

4. Which animal squeaks through its nose?

5. Which animal has glowing eyes?

1. Scorpion 2. Loris 3. Raccoon 4. Bat 5. Leopard